About the Author

Stephanie Latham is a rather eccentric English teacher from the north west of England. She currently resides with her husband, twin daughters, and his Lordship TK the cat. She has more books than she knows what to with and plays Dungeons and Dragons with her friends several times a week. Mostly, she's trying to be a 'serious adult', whatever that means.

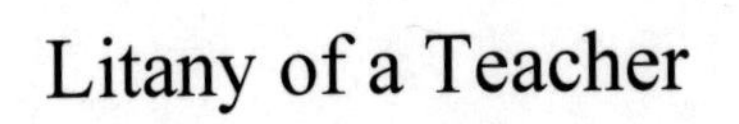

Stephanie Latham

Litany of a Teacher

Vanguard Press

VANGUARD PAPERBACK

A CIP catalogue record for this title is available from the British Library.

ISBN 978 1 80016 695 0

Vanguard Press is an imprint of
Pegasus Elliot Mackenzie Publishers Ltd.
www.pegasuspublishers.com

First Published in 2024

Vanguard Press
Sheraton House Castle Park
Cambridge England

Printed & Bound in Great Britain

Dedication

For my family and friends – forever my font of inspiration

Acknowledgements

I'd like to acknowledge my husband, Jp, for being so actively supportive and helping me figure out a way for this dream to come true, for always being my motivation and for soothing my sleep-addled brain. I would also like to acknowledge Dr Ranaa Bokhari, Caroline Turner, Allyson Phillips, my daughters, Evelyn and Isabelle, and all my colleagues for being such inspirational people- and for giving me plenty of material to write about.

Contents

A Moral Quandary

I find myself asking
'Who decides if we are good?'
Is it the lawman, or the poor man?
The butcher, baker or candlestick maker?

When we protest 'I'm a good person!'
Do we decide that what we are,
Is good,
That all good people should look like
Us?
Or do we simply not want to be like 'the bad'
People
We're not like them. We're good.

Does God decide?
If so, what are the criteria?
'Well, you prayed on Sundays, Jimmy, so you're all paid up
Here'
Or is it
'Well, you kept the sabbath, Sam, but you didn't give a damn
About your fellow man,
You're stuck, old mucker.'

How do we see the black and white

Through sunglass shades of grey?

And I decide it's too early
To be pondering this moral quandary
Before the coffee
First thing on a Monday.

A Sonnet for My Husband

My love has eyes like icebergs in the sea
Shining in the salt, they glow cool and bright
My love has ginger hair, creative and free
He is fiery comfort, a living spice.
My love's laugh is loud, it cuts through the air,
A bubbling joy, a vibrant light so clear.
My love's mind is as silver, keen and rare,
A wit so quick and sharp, a lightning spear.
My love's heart, sometimes a towering shield,
Is soft for me, warm safe, a knitted nest
And though the years have change and scars revealed
I love each wrinkled mark, memories blessed.
My love and I grow careworn, old and grey,
And I love him the same as the first day.

Another Realm

The front door slams
As she leaves her teacher's garb behind
And instead, evolves
She dons a pirate's hat,
Sugar-skull paint
Or a feathered fan
And enters
Another realm

She smiles at her comrades,
Through the shine of a screen,
But really, they're present
Their arms linked
Together against the rising tide

With them, she has swum in crystal-coloured streams
Trailed evergreen forests, struggled
Through cold mountain passes
She's hunted dragons, great beings of old tales
Terrifying – but not as chilling as the day-to-day
Nightmare

She laughs at them.
All they take,
Is a roll of the dice.
And they are gone.

She sings made-up songs
In make-believe taverns
And makes conversation
With imaginary companions

As the next day dawns, and the cardigan returns
Armed with a hip flask of caffeine and hope
She has to wonder
Which part of her is really
The character?

Body Parts

I gave myself away today.
Oh, not all at once, you understand.
Someone asked me for a hand, so
I gave my left. I don't use that one much.
Someone asked me to put my ear to the ground.
So I did, and left it there.
Someone asked me to eyeball something,
To give it a look over.
So I gave them my eyes.
(Joke's on them though, they forgot the glasses)
Someone took my breath away
Pity it was still in my lungs
Some handsome bugger stole my heart
Someone else gave me a penny for my thoughts
Someone told me I should walk a mile in their shoes
So I gave them my feet
Someone told me to hold my tongue
Someone else told me to hold my nose
Someone wanted my blood
(They didn't want the sweat or tears that came with it)
Someone wanted a leg up
Someone wanted a good old knees-up too.
I gave someone a shoulder to cry on
And a belly full of laughs
Someone said I had no backbone
'No,' I said, 'I gave it away!'

And so I'm left with the rest of me
And I wonder why
I feel
Empty.

Bomb

There's a bomb inside my chest.
Just inside my ribs, tucked above my stomach.
I can feel it fizzing away, trembling,
Ticking.
The fuse is in my brain.
It travels down the back of my neck—
I can't see it
But I feel its quivering string,
The travelling, burning heat.
I try to push the bomb down,
Heavy roundness in my belly
It's cold, like a cannonball
But furiously hot, too.
I keep pushing, try to smother
Try to keep myself together.
But the spark from my brain pushes faster.
Faster.
There'll be a
BOOM
Any second now.

Candidate Regiment

Line by line, chattering – then stop
About to go over
The top
Weapons ready, biro swords and ruler shields
The clicking of rifles
The panic stifles
Wide eyed, staring, helpless
Like frightened horses.
Stand to attention
To tension
To all that hangs in the balance
We wish it was us
In the exam hall, instead of them
As we wave them off
With one final salute
They march towards no man's land
And are gone.

Classroom Symphony

Shuffle, shuffle, tap, tap.
The conductor coughs, and raises the baton
Cogs whirr
Pens click
Opinions clash (like paint, only louder)
Palms slam
Zips hiss
Pencils scritch
Markers squeak
Teachers frown in a deafening expression
Laptops chitter chatter
Rain pitter patters
Pages flitter flutter
Voices recite, reread, repeat
Ideas flow
Learning grows into a crescendo
And then the bell goes.
The door is closed.
Silence falls.
A sigh.

Help Me, I'm Drowning.

I fall slowly, sinking through the space
The black canvas of the deep
No life surrounds me
No shimmering shoals or silent sharks
Not even coral or shells to speak of
Only a simple strip of moonlight
Dim, to remind me of the light
I struggle against the dark blue,
Pushing at the water like moving my hands
Through wisps of material
I suffocate, gasping in the cold,
But I can't swim out.
I keep trying to reach the surface
Crack it like ice or glass
My arms burn as I flail, my lungs feel like they're trying
to crawl out of my mouth
To save themselves
As the water pulls me down
Pulling,
Pulling,
Pulling.
Into the blackness, unable to breathe free
Unable to breathe.

Diverging Paths

I stood at a crossroads
Down one path, there was you.
You were smiling, with a wide heart
Bare, strong arms and tired eyes – handsome
I could see you in the distance.
You were silent, grey.
You stumbled towards me, slowly,
Always glancing around, distracted by the haze.

We carried our own dreams, you and I.
Bundled up like a picnic in a checked blanket.
I had the map – I was always better organised
More surefooted, direct,
Unlike your dreamy exploration.
The other path was hidden,
Shrouded in a mist – I heard laughter,
Bells, the shrieking of children,
The clinking of glasses, the ruckus
Of Christmas songs, of Happy Birthdays
And something seemed to glow,
Brightly glow.

I turned back to you, sad
To see you had stopped, you were unpacking your bundle.
I waited a while, but the laughter
And the glow drew me onward.

I'm sorry, I had to leave you behind – my own bundle grew
heavy.
I felt you tug at my heart-string, once, twice,
But I pulled away, and you were lost.
From time to time I think,
As I laugh and clink my glass,
Of you, and wonder
Whether you found your own glow.

Dollface

The bathroom mirror stares back
The white gleam of the porcelain face
Stares back at me
The snow-perfect skin
Icicle eyes, feathered eyelashes
Red lips glistening like cherries
Fresh as a spring morning, dew dropped.
Grin plastered into place, as if with hooks
I turn to face the day.
It protects my paper skin
Won't let the stormy words in
Smiles surround me.
They see the porcelain-perfect
They smile back, satisfied.
At home, I untie the elastic ribbon that keeps the face in check.
It slips, reveals
The clownish frown beneath
And I can see the cracks, a split
Into the darkness.

Dollface Part Two

The picture-perfect porcelain is so cold
Cold to the touch, cold on my skin
The painted lips are hard, fixed into place
I have to keep the darkness in
Behind the eyes of glass
Are monsters
Vampires, leeches, creatures waiting
They mimic me, cruelly mocking
A distorted mirror
Just for a second, the mask
slips
I catch it, reattach it
But they have seen the light
But they have seen the dark
I paper over the cracks,
Hastily, haphazard patch job
'Everything's fine,' I say
But they've seen the cracks now.
Today my face is stronger
The glistening porcelain, bleach white,
Thicker. Perfect.
My lips are brighter,
chemical cherry bomb
My cheeks are lighter
A sickly cupcake pink
And the eyes of glass

Blue marbled, mirrored pools of water
They show nothing except who’s looking
I wear my face extra tight
Maybe I’ll convince them
I’m all right

Dr Raana Bokhari

She carries her faith
Like a beacon – a flashing buoy
A saviour to the sea-tossed, a sign of salvation.

She carries her faith
Like a lantern on a Shepherd's crook
To light the way for the lost and lonely.

She carries her faith
Like a homely, flickering fireplace
For the forgotten, full of warmth and forgiveness

She carries her faith
Like a soft evening candle
Kindness shines, come and eat with me!

She carries her faith
Like a green desk lamp
Illuminating scriptures, enlightened and intelligent.

She carries her faith
Like a lighted staff
Graceful dignity, humble modesty.

She carries her faith
Like a flaming torch

Shining into place where light is needed most.
Her faith leaves a glow behind,
A legacy of light.

Edukashun

We don’t need no maths books
Or past books, or this is what a good answer
Looks like
We don’t need no essays or canteen trays
Lunchtime stays or ‘education pays’ stuff
No teachers teaching, preaching
To us like we need it
We don’t need no reading or pleading
For help, we’re too cool
For that dealing, that teacher’s pet squealin’.
We need street cred, popularity instead
Pop stars and rock stars
Instagram pics, that’s what’s sick
We need the he said she said, going to bed
At four am, I’ll sleep when
I’m dead lark
We need good looks and right hooks
Trends and time with friends
You know, the stuff what matters
And a plaster, for when we scrape our knees
and cry
cos we’re upset
When we find out
just how hard
life gets

Empty

Once a year, we empty ourselves out.
Like an old pencil case, we shake out
The old shavings, broken promise pencil nibs
And general lint of anger, frustration.
We give our souls a spring clean.

Afterwards, we feel as empty as space
The lack of cluttering day-to-day problems
Making the inside of us feel evermore weightless,
Incomplete.
We make space for forgiveness, shiny and new
And when we fill again, with love and remembrance
Warm as fresh bread,
We inhale gratitude. We are thankful for the space
For the time to spring clean, for the time to turn the mirror on ourselves
For the chance to remember what will never come, and to whom.
For yet another chance to polish ourselves, buffing out the too-wrong dents
That we've made.

Ready to face what comes with smiling grace
To embrace the unknown clean, like a fresh linen sheet.
To breathe a sigh of relief.

Endlessly Chasing

Through the void we stumble,
Pushing blindly
To the sparkle of light beyond
It used to surround us
Basking in its warmth, we felt it
Cold
Then all was dark.
Voices trail,
Echoes of life, drifting away like a boat
Unanchored from its mooring, floating
Out into the black sea.
We don't know where we are,
Or where WE are.
All there is, is the pinprick beam
Gleaming, like a torch shining
Through a keyhole.
We stumble forward, it moves further away
With each
Clumsy
Step.

First day at school
I stand at the front gates,
Shivering.
They're all so big, all these others.
Pupils.

They walk with the world on their shoulders, tall and proud.
The air filled with dignified learning.
I don't think I'm ready.

A gaggling whirlwind whooshes past,
Ruffling my new clothes,
But my new shoes hold me fast
Booted to the ground.

I sigh.
I didn't want to go to school today.
But they said I had to.
When I asked 'why?'
They said—
'Because you're the teacher.'

Flying

The birds are going to fly today.
They've been trying for months,
Stretching their wings, flexing sinew
Testing out the feathers,
Adjusting to the wind's push
They wobble, taking shaking steps
Towards the edge
Eyes glittering, flicking
Between the nest,
Soft, supporting, safe
Towards the unknown horizon
The shining skyline of stars and scrapers
The time comes for each to
Leap!
They scatter like dandelion seeds,
Fleeing, floating, flying free
A blanket of colour spreading
To make the world
More hopeful
I smile at their futures.

Gone

There's an empty chair where I should be
A violet tranquillity, soothing soul
The squeezing, crushing pressure of the table
Vanished into vacancy.

There's an empty silence where words should be
Contemplative quiet, calm collective
The cacophony of cauterising voices
Now a serene softness

There's an empty space where weight should be
A light; an airy, aviary freedom
The punitive, piercing pain, self-inflicted
Now cold and clear

There's an empty place where a burden once was
Radiant relief, a breath, a sigh
The bouldering, bothersome thorn
Removed: now throbbing ripples

There's a stillness where movement should be
A mournful meditation, blue serenity
The fuzzy, furious frantic
Now a mirrored glass, a flat surface
There's a whiteness where red should be
Fresh and blank, like lilies

The rushing, ruddy anger of life
Slowly ebbing away, now pure nothingness

Me in My Box

It gets lonely in my box.
The silence is deafening,
Wrapped around my head
Constrictor-like squeezing
It's cold here. The walls
Are stiff and unforgiving
'WORK!' they repeat
Flat and lifeless.
Then comes the tap, tap, tapping
Like a child's fingers on a fish bowl
Swirling the water around and around
It makes me dizzy.

I look up, to the soft sky above.
Little cherubs in soft pink glows
Rest carefully on cloudy pillows,
Or else watch life pass by.
I sigh, oh! To be a part of the warmth
The pastel-coloured music, the comfort
And the soft cotton sleep.

But it is not for me.
I return to the dark walls of my box
The silence, the tapping, and stamp my feet
Trying to stave off the cold inside.
The chill creeps ever inwards.

Mother

She trudges, slowly, to the front door
Weighed down with bags.
She puffs, takes a moment to pause
And compose.
A calmness appears, before she opens.
Opens the doors,
Opens her arms,
Opens her smile,
Opens her heart.
Irradiating warmth, like a cooking pot of kindness
A soft glow surrounds her, like candlelight.
Her skin is a tableau, a mosaic of memories
Troubles and triumphs, telling tales.
Her children give blank looks
Or else tug on her sleeve, desperate
To show her what they've done today
They are enveloped in her love.
Sometimes they adventure out,
Testing the churning waters,
But always returning
Home.

My Thumbs

My thumbs are a mess
My fingernails pick mindlessly
Incessantly
Like jagged hooks they claw
Tear the flesh.
Dried blood marks yesterday's battles
And the skin, a no man's land,
Is gouged with fresh scars
It peaks and troughs with rough edges
Like ripped paper
The only outward sign
Of the internal struggle.
My poor thumbs take the brunt
They can't hide the pain
Not like my face can.

Puppet

Strings tied around my elbows, I jerk
Crumple and tumble, limbs akimbo
A round face, pink circles for cheeks
Sea-blue button eyes, shiny,
Cheap plastic.

I tilt my head towards the crowd
My wide mouth opens and closes like a butterfly's wings
The words form like bubbles, pop in front of their eyes
Parts of my soul emerging from my cotton lips.
They laugh, mocking the stuffing under my rope hair
Or else pay no attention.

Who would listen to the puppet girl
With a head full of black, stormy fluff?
Who listens to a soul smothered
In straw and hessian?

One little boy reaches up
Gently strokes my raggedy head
Stares into the coldness of my plastic eyes
Can he see me? Can he hear me?
Does he hear me?
I'm screaming inside, my chest burns,
The smouldering magma rising up my throat
HEAR ME!

But my painted face remains stiff, felt soft,
Plaited strings and painted rosiness
The little boy seems satisfied with the façade
And laughs away
Like the rest.

No tears from my plastic eyes
I go on
Crumpling and tumbling,
To indifferent laughter and derisive glances
Until the fire dies
And nothing but blue button eyes, plastic, remain.
There's nothing left
Of me

September

You are flung – Rudely
Out of the warm sizzle of sunshine
Into the drizzle, and dreary grey half dream
The indifferent cold metal of the cabinet waits for you.
You stumble
Feet fumbling, trying to outrun
The ground, as it rumbles and pulls beneath
Your feet, like a treadmill
You fall. You roll.
You knew this was coming, but like a petulant child
You turned away, desperately clinging
To the breezy, bright coolness of August
You turned back to the clinking of ice cubes in the glass
And the crisp liberation.
It seems so long ago now.
You roll, dirty snow gathering around you
Balling up like a frightened hedgehog
You gather momentum, bewildered
Blundering around in the twilight
The snow around you gathers, paper white
Rolling, rolling.
Trapped inside, you pray
For the soft trunk
Of Halloween, or Christmas
To break the icy tomb.

Teacher

We sit
The time bomb on the wall ticks
Like the ones inside our
HEAD.
Reports are due – but whose?
Theirs? It's all a blur
Smiling faces try – but these aren't the enemies
We face
Alone
Striving to help those who don't think
They need it.
They fight us, cut us deep with their frustrated indifference
like shards of ice.
We stand.
Our eyes have seen the world, the blinding darkness
We cannot shield them, like lambs to the slaughter
Their exposure is inevitable.
We must train them, prepare them, arm them against the coming
Horrors.
Give them eyes to see past the dark,
To see beauty
Give them hands to move past the war
To create kindness
Give them hearts to feel past the anger
To create love.

Some listen; some learn. Some prepare.
Some fight us like toddlers,
Pushing and screaming against the tide.
The feelings mix like a cauldron, molten and hot
First red, then pink, then blue and green
And back to red
All an artist's palette
Mixing
But we must separate.
Be a blank slate
Before the tolling of the school bell rings.

The Dragon

Smoke curls around the doorway,
A dangerous invitation, stifling
You don't want to enter, Miss.
Here be a dragon.

Fiercely she guards her treasure,
Black scales gleam like inky fish
Tails swishing, straining for safety,
Iron claws grip and curl around the hoard.

A pile of tribute keeps warm her lair,
Bound tomes are soft, offer stories of comfort from the cold
The pages whisper to her, words twisting,
Dancing around her dragon's brain.
Grey tentacles, tendrils of terrible inferno emerge from flaring nostrils
Magma inside her chest, it flares and flickers
Fire!
Red flames fill her form,
Fury.

Fiercely she guards her eggs,
Her greatest treasure
Waiting, ever waiting, a patient ember.
Waiting for the tell-tale crack, tap-tap-tapping
For the fire to begin again

The Lioness

She stalks the sun-bleached yellow land
Even the proudest lion, their manes fluffed
Won't meet her gaze, and shrink back
From her path.

Through the crowds she prowls,
Herding the cubs, all of them her children,
guiding them
Outward, towards the open savannah,
Towards the bright horizon, the blazing orange sun
Her lessons yet ringing in their ears;
'Hunt, chase, lead,' she whispers.

And when a challenger comes,
Prowling, snarling, snapping, insidious
Her sharpened maw bares her point
A claw snatches, she strikes, circling
Until the loser slinks silently away,
Wounded.
She stands firm, a stalwart sentinel
Defending her Pride against the sneering tide
The pack at her side; she takes point
A flaming torch through the darkness
Of a concrete jungle
And corridor rivers.

The Owl

High up on his perch, he sits
Amongst the bristling branches grips
The bough beneath him, piercing gaze
Focus through the foggy haze
In quiet repose, he observes
The world beneath, somewhat unnerves
The creatures swarming, buzzing below
He guards them here; and here they grow
Wise wings spread, warm winds surround
The eager creatures on the ground
But calmness covers, like the shade
Cooling tranquil, noises fade
The owl, eyes wide, proudly stands
Wise heart, kind words, open hands
A guardian of the forest flies
Between the earth and starry skies

For Shenaz

From her high glass perch, she watches
Softly purring, listening, vigilant
Her jewellery catches the light
Sparking, like sunlight on a tropical ocean
Gossip whispers as she climbs down,
The clinking of china cups and crumbs,
The smell of coffee
And sweet perfume trails
She is soft,
But regal in her furs
Like a Persian cat, clever
But still a comfort,
Confident in her company,
Fluffy slippers and diamonds
Bejewelled claws extend
Offer up a warm cup
And a biscuit
Her sharp eyes shine
Beneath a heartfelt smile.

The P

It forms, in my head
A floating ball of moulding, bubbling clay
Centred in my in my chest

I need to get it out.
It moves to my tongue,
A soft flame, burning just
Around the edges.
Words flick and flutter
Around my eyes like birds
Diving and ascending
Flitting in and out of vision faster than I can think
I'm unable to catch them.
I'm frustrated.
I need to get it out, but the words
Won't behave
Won't lie on the page and convey
Not like I want them to.

The clay begins to form
Vocabulary sculpting, scraping and gouging
The tools of my trade, carving out my meaning
Fingers itch, twitch
With purpose and life
The clay turns to water, flowing
Up, up from my centre,

Up, up to head,
Through the cavern of my mouth
Down, down my arms, my fingers
Through the black abyss of ink
Where you can fish
For my
Ideas.

The Ringmaster

Roll up, roll up, come and see
The Ringmaster!
Marvel at kaleidoscope colours
And harlequin movement!
Watch as she juggles!
Spinning plates on wobbling sticks, and somehow
She keeps spinning, spinning,
Swirling, never stopping in place
She keeps them all aloft, smiling
Her tales will amaze!
Nothing can quench the fire of her
Mind; it's catching, the flames
Engulfing the audience around her
The fire is in their eyes now too.
What now? Death-defying odds?
The tightrope twangs, but she balances
Perfectly, her pretty parasol poised
Above the crocodile tank.
Incredible!
She takes her bow, silver smile shining,
Falters only for a flicker,
As she remembers
She must do it all again tomorrow.

The World Beyond

Loud white noise surrounds the air
Harsh crows, chatter clinks and taps
But all sounds begin to blur beneath the pressure of the paper
Like plunging your head under water
The soft flip
The warm hearth of words, beating softly
Beckoning to a world beyond.
'Escape in me,', the ghostly pages whisper.
Vain fantasies, stories that grip and curl, complex emotions captured
In a simple, comforting binding.
Lives twisted together, they seep into my mind like ink trails through water
Like breathing, living.
When it ends, I grieve
The world is over, the world continues to spin
The ordinary noise returns, the clinks and taps
But to me, it just feels
Wrong.

They Didn't Touch Her

Shik!
Another cut splits the skin
Droplets of blood rise, form like gemstones
A whisper.
Whump!
Another ball to the gut,
Pushing the insides up and out
Aching.
A sneer.
Crackle!
Head hits concrete, crunches
Eyes swell like a child's party balloon
A snigger
Whack!
A kick to the ribs, piercing
Something red spatters the pavement
A word.
HISSS!
Skin burns, almost cold.
Searing pain and the smell of burning meat.
A shaking of a head, fingers rolling in a loop
At the temple
Guttering.
The constrictor hands pull tighter
Choking, crushing.
She can't breathe.

She stands,
Bloodied. Beaten. Betrayed.
Broken.
But not a mark on her paper skin.
They didn't touch her.

They Turn Their Backs

I beg, I plead.
'I care!' I shout
But they turn their backs
I strive, I exhaust,
I stretch myself thin like the paper they use
I lift, I pull up, straining.
But they turn their backs
I laugh and cry
With them, for them,
I bleed my best
But still, in the end
They turn their backs.
Sometimes in my dream
They smile, they help themselves
They work with me
But eventually
They all turn their backs.

Time

What time is it?
Time to get up
Time to eat, time to leave
Time for work,
Train times, deadlines
The clock ticks, a time bomb.
Time for a break, but not when it's
Time to support, mentor
Time to rectify,
Time to teach, time to preach
Tea time? No time
For that now
Home time. Trains again,
Can't stop and chat, no time!
Hope all is well.
Time to go! Time to shop
Before it's closing time.
My watch is a blur.
Time for a shower.
Time for bed.
As we lay there at night, staring at the blank ceiling
We wonder
Where all the time went.

Unfinished

I can feel myself ebbing away
Like paint, too diluted
Once a shock of rich teal, electric blue
Now faded, the colour swirling
Turning pale as an evening sky
I feel the holes opening up within me
Like a slice of bread pecked by birds
Sharp beaks and claws tearing
Shredding, ripping. .
The gulls all taking their share
Of me.
I fade away into the background
The buzzing drowns out my whispers
As I'm pushed back, I am uninteresting
Dulled by static. I bore them. I am pushed
Out.

You Are the World

You are a tempest,
Ever changing, a broiling bubbling cauldron
Of deep cloud and slate grey thunder.
Shaking the heavens.
You are a tornado,
Endless, effortless destruction
Sweeping away into the distance
Leaving a trail of squealing, screaming noise
And barren, broken land.

You are the sun
A warm, glowing orb of brightest joy
Laughter erupting like flares, spurts of magma
A gentle heat, like hot soup on a winter afternoon.

You are a galaxy
An infinity of stars, firing and connecting and blinking
In the chasm of space behind your eyes
Spinning the concentrated web of new thoughts, new things
New you

You are an earthquake
Cracking, snapping all that came before
Shaking loose the stale cobwebs, rustling routines and stagnation

Leaving the world in a trembling daze, but blank
Wiped clean like bleached marble
as if to start again
Anew.

Borderline Rant

Somewhere, sometime,
Somebody drew a line and said
'You can't cross that, it's mine'
And then other tribes said, 'Fine.
You can't come here either,
We own this bit.'
And so more lines were drawn over time
More borders born across the lands
Lines drawn in the sand to signify
Division, separation,
And if lines were crossed, well, retaliation
And people grew apart, at the start
Things might have been okay but then, selfishness
Caught on, and greed grew like a weed and took over
Enveloped and we grew colder
Inside, and wanted more,
More land, more resources, more sources
To prove we were superior – we sailed
With ulterior motives, offered a hand
But pulled the swords from behind as we took
The land, pulled the rug out
From under each other – waged war
Because we thought we belonged, that we
Were born better, we set our sights
On other's homes, their rights,
And we blinded ourselves to what's right because

We believed we WERE right. We were white
Which made us… what?
Invaders. Degraders. Erasers of history and culture.
And I mourn what we could have learned, the trust and fellowship we could have earned
The beauty that could have been. I yearn for it.
But now is the time, to rewind – to remind ourselves
Of the colours of the world
To share what we have, our privilege
To dust off the covers of our history books and recover
What was lost – return what was taken, re-write the narration and learn
From each other. To celebrate, appreciate
The differences, variety is the spice of life, they say,
So why do we wish our countries to stay the same?
Like white chicken, white rice, no flavour, mundane!
'You can't come over here'
"This is our land our place"
It wasn't given or earned, we just decided
To take it with blood, and a grand gesture of
"education". When will we come to the realization,
That white does not equal right, and show some appreciation
For the nations and peoples we destroyed in the name
Of so called "Civilization"?
Well, I'm done being bland. Welcome to my table,
Welcome to our land. I offer my hand, let's share
What we have. I acknowledge the wrongs done to you
By me, and mine.

I can't give back blood, or life, or time, but I can fight for
What's rightfully yours – respect, dignity, your God(s) given right
To be treated with humility, sincerity
To be treated as another human soul, not a stranger
Crossing an invisible line drawn thousands of years ago
Or being on the side we wanted, because the grass was greener.
Your identity is beautiful.
I'm sorry we took it away for so long. We were wrong.

Cherry Blossoms

Every Spring, the cherry blossoms
Burst into life.
Soft and gentle,
The marshmallow sunrise pink
Surrounds us in a susurrus of serenity
The wind whispering secrets in between branches
Like secluded lovers
Too soon, they fall
Petal confetti at a wedding
Like pastel snow
They drift, as if through water
Fluttering finally to the pavement
Dying before the sun sets
The end of spring warmth
We hold on to the blossom hope,
Waiting eagerly once a year
Before our dreams go to die once more.

Unnamed

I can feel your tendrils
Like smoke given substance, they wrap
Around my beating heart, my brain, my belly
Your fingers are always there, lurking
Stroking the back of my mind, down my spine
During the day, I can bat you away
And you shrink, sneering
Content to wait. You let me be,
For now.
Later, you open one eye
Yellow, piercing, baring all and blaring
Like a siren
Your pastel woollen threads surround me
The bright smoke comforting, controlling, constricting
I am mesmerised, immobile
Paralysed by you – but I don't protest.
I love and hate you.

Karen

Ahem
AHEM
Excuse me, Governments?
World Leaders, United Nations,
God?
I'd like to see the manager.
No, right now.
You see, I have a problem with the world.
This country is defective – it murders people who love.
This one isn't much better – it murders culture and religion.
(Often by those who are SUPPOSED to protect. Isn't that horrifically ironic?)
And there are several that poison us. And don't get me started
On women! Some of us can't drive – can't learn – can't live. It murders us.
Is it supposed to do that?
No, I didn't think so.
So you see, I'd like to see a manager.
I want to know what you're going to do about these problems.
There are so many.
No, you don't understand – I am a middle-aged white woman,

With a career, two blue-eyed children and a driving license.
You HAVE to listen to me.
Don't make me call my husband; you don't want him involved!
Yes, I thought as much.
No, I don't want credit. I don't want a refund – I don't need it.
We want this one exchanged – changed
We need one without so many lines being crossed.
Can you have that arranged?

Last Halloween

Last Halloween, it happened.
I'm not sure how – I just know that I was walking home
Through the puddles, and the rain, and the thunder
Through the tunnel under the road
The graffitied mural mosaic mocking me, pointing out the decay
And then came the blood.
I never understood that part.
A gash blossomed across the softness of my belly,
Split like a pod, glistening.
Another into my breast, piercing,
Drawing out the essence of life like a tap.
My back too, then my legs.
I lay bleeding against the walls of the tunnel.
Ribbons streaming from a fountain centre.
A clown passes by, then a cat,
A policeman, a nurse, a fireman,
A builder, a vampire, a ghost
All turn to look
At me; all smile.
All giggle at my great costume.
I try to protest, clinging longingly to a paling hope.
Like a rope attached to a well-bucket, running through burning fingers
But my 'performance' is too convincing, too cunning
They see through my 'disguise' to the 'reality' beneath

“She’s not really hurt – it’s Halloween, hurrah!
The fake blood is a great touch, really lifelike
I wonder where she got the prosthetics from?
That wound almost looks real!”
Slowly, slowly, I fade away,
To become tomorrow’s headline—
And they’ll say they had ‘no idea’
I was bleeding.

My Little Boat and I

We are out at sea,
My little boat and I.
It was calm when we ventured out
Into the calm blue abyss
We couldn't see the storm on the horizon
Looming, looming.
Now I am lost somewhere,
Somewhere.
My little boat has splintered and cracked
Like a porcelain teacup that's bashed
Too hard against teeth and tongues and teapots
Every time I look up to the storm
Try to get some bearings or balance,
Some semblance of the somewhere that I am
The ocean explodes
Shoves itself into my mouth and down my throat
And I can't breathe
Sometimes, I find comfort in bottles
Messages of warmth, of soothing, scalding heat
But they fizzle out and die
When the next wave comes crushing down
I hope to see the sun again someday,
But every day
A little more
Is washed
Away.

On the Cliffs

I stand on a cliff edge,
Staring into the abyss below
The white, rocky cliffs stained
With albatross
And blood
Below, the water churns
Like blue butter, frothing at the mouth
Hungry, with jagged teeth
It beckons me to jump.
My feet hang over the precipice,
Half in the air, floating
Half anchored in safety.
I glance back towards the warm safety of the trees.
I know each bark, branch and twig,
Each knot, cluster and gnarled root
Each leaf, hole and burrow.
I know it all, I.
I turn back to the wide, empty world.
The wind ruffles my feathers with uncertainty
I stick one foot over the edge, balancing now,
Swaying, teetering, almost
Almost
I step into the air
And wait to see if I fly.

Paris

You were grumpy with me that day;
It was blisteringly hot and crowded,
We were thirsty, and you were tired.
It made me sad.
But when we crossed the bridge, what a sight we saw!
Fountains of blue opals, spitting treasure into the sky
Caught by sunlight, drops of blessed water
Clicked into rainbow diamonds, and were caught
By laughing children.
As if waking from a dream, we ran.
Your socks were off first, and in you went,
Splashing, wading, while I sat at the edge dangling my feet,
Smiling at your pigtails.
We found a better spot,
And then we were both in. I held my skirt
To one side, for some modesty—
But we laughed so loud, like we were teenagers again.
We posed in front of the Eiffel Tower,
Two divas, striking at the world, looking silly
But feeling like a million euros. We took pictures,
Artfully – at least in your case!
It's funny – when I look back,
I barely remember your grumpiness,
Your scowl is shaded over by your summer smile.

Pinball

The dawn pulls back,
Pulling, pulling, pulling…
ZING!
RING!
The alarm shoots you up and awake,
Like a bullet, you hit the ground
Running, half-stunned, the sounds coming around
Toaster pops, the car unlocks, the shock
Of the horn in the traffic, the static
Of your jumper pricks. It's too quick
You feel sick, but there's no time
To stop now. You clock in,
Take stock of your desk, then comes the PING, off the walls,
The computer sings to life, emails wing, the phone rings
There are meetings and greetings and please-have-a-seat-ings
The paper piles in, the pressure building, pressed to pulp
It flies out again, paper planes delivering business.
The coffee drains; refills; drains; refills,
Launches you up again as you tumble,
Then bang – you're shoved
Out the door, pedal to the floor
And you're home, but there's more to do yet.
Washing and chopping, cleaning and feeding
Making deals and compromising,

Occasionally the anger rises, you want to dive away,
Pry the grey tiredness away, you pass
Each other like ships in the night
You're not sure what's right or wrong or left
But you shelf it, deal with it later.
You're finally ushered, dented and dealt with
Scuffed, you shuffle and fall into bed, and rest.
The dawn pulls back…

Powerful Mother

Her blood boils the rocks beneath the earth,
Sluggishly drags down the dwellings of men,
Slurping up skyscrapers with viscous, simmering stone.
Her tears freeze the mountains, rivers, lakes
A thousand years they say it takes,
For her icy water to reach the pools in her wake.
Her anger erupts,
A geyser explosion, a hissing spit
Then gone again, bubbling below,
Steaming, sinister.
Sometimes we forget her—
Like arrogant peacocks, we show off what we think
Is power, wealth – fabricated, a fake.
She created us, moulded us, watched us grow in the cradle
of the earth
She reminds us, sometimes,
With hurricanes and terror,
That really,
We are nothing.

Rome

I remember where you proposed.
I don't remember the day, or the week,
Or what was in the news at the time.
But I remember where it happened.
The sunlight covered everything,
A stifling blanket that we hid underneath,
Like children. We sought relief with ice cream.
Light made the fountain glow, radiant,
Divine, as if from Olympus itself.
The smooth marble figures watched us,
Oceanus, Triton, Agrippa,
Infallible, Ineffable,
Overflowing with topaz aqua vita.
I thought it beautiful, the overabundance
Of fruits and fertility.
Little did I know—
You were on one knee, shaking,
And I was shaking too.
Before the Pantheon, I agreed.
We weren't children playing at love any more.

Sea Woman

Once upon a time,
There was a woman adrift at sea.
Sometimes, it was calm.
And her little boat floated on a glass mirror.
The sun was gentle and warm,
And she was able to fish.

But more often than not,
The waves loomed, large and ominous
Black mountain peaks, bullying the little boat
Unleashing anger unfelt, crushing and smashing
Still she held onto her sail, pulling on the safety ropes
Fighting against the bonds of disaster, clinging still.

Occasionally, she would come across a sailor,
Another sea-stained shipwreck,
And she offered succour, safe harbour,
An oar to use as they sailed away,
As she smiled sadly at her solitude.

In the distance, she could see an island.
A small speck of salvation, a single shining spotlight of
sun,
On the last hint of the horizon.
She knew that her little boat would carry her,
Exhausted, drained of all but the dregs of determination,

Towards the glimmering paradise,
And with furtive tugs of fortitude,
She continues
On, on, on.

Not That Kind of Poet

When I say I'm a poet
People say,
'Oh! Like Shakespeare!'
The steady stage set with sobriety,
Sombre sonnets, each iamb puncturing pentameter.
Comparing lovers to summer days,
Considering life's great questions,
Of being, or not being, like a metaphysical,
Philosophical practitioner of perfected performance
And abject eloquence.
Chasing metaphors for the cheers of the audience?
I'm not that sort of poet.

When I say I'm a poet
People say,
'Oh! Like Wordsworth!'
Daydreaming, dancing with the daffodils
Along the lake edge, daring to tempt
The mountain, the peaks uprearing,
The comfort of the cardigan cottage dwarfed by the romantic,
The sublimity of nature; the swishing waves,
Swooping swallows and doves,
Yet somehow troubled; emotions tossing
The little boat, bobbing like a cork?
I'm not that sort of poet.

When I say I'm a poet
People say,
'Oh! Like Angelou!'
Challenging injustice,
An angel with a flaming sword,
Fire woman, with worn shoes
And a worn smile, her skin scarred and beautiful.
She towers, as powerful as Poseidon,
Pulling in the tide, leaving me in awe
Like a gaping fisherwoman.
She is anger and fury, activism spreading
CONFIDENCE?
I'm not that sort of poet.

When I say I'm a poet
People say,
'Oh! Like Rosetti!'
Telling tales of Goblin men,
Of sucking fruits, of woodland glens
Of sacrificing sister's sweet
Redeeming hands and summer heat
Of violent beauty, temptation's door
Of fallen women, of sin and flaw
Of youth and beauty, mother's milk
Of golden hair as smooth as silk?
I'm not that kind of poet.

When I say I'm a poet,

I mean I'm a bad rappin', free-fallin' deep-divin',
Metaphorical, allegorical, emotional oracle,
Puppet-master, twisting and turning the words
I make them dance to MY tune, wrap them around
My tongue, my fingers.
I'm a ball of molten fire, a wisp of silk in water,
I'm the drum beat and the trumpet,
I'm the violin's mournful cry and the funky jazz tune.
I am rigid structure and
Sometimes
None at all.
I'm THAT kind of poet.

The Tornado

WHOOSH!
A whizzing stream of black chiffon crashes into the building
It storms down the corridor, papers whirling, flapping
Erratically in the bellowing of the wind.
Footsteps rumble like thunder,
Like palpitations of the Heart.
A crescendo of dignity and respect draws up.
The eyes of the hurricane are wide; searching,
Like spotlights for trouble.
There is a grace in the power of the storm.

The World is Broken

Dust and ash puff out of newspaper prints
In clouds of suffocating suffering.
Inside the pictures, children
Cannot breathe. They stand silently
Motionless, gasping against the ink-clogged air.
They are reflected in glass business lenses.
Blood oozes from television screens
Men trapped inside, boxed in
By molten fury, desperate.
It trickles out of the man's mouth like flaming treacle
The last globule of life drips down the television screen
And onto the ivory living room carpet.
Cracks echo through the voices in the street
Cries of cold innocence are pushed, pushed,
Herded into concrete confines like cattle
Rattled by the shrieking of rifles and rockets
Pushed out, pushed out.
Then silence, as the world breaks.
Without pause,
They plaster over the cracks, hide them from anyone who
  glances past.
But if you look, my friend, you'll see
The dark chasm shining beneath the papered wall.
The world is broken.

Travelling

You grin up at me,
Your four teeth barely visible,
Concentration etched
Into every smooth crevice of your skin.
Your sister sits in my lap
And watches, lying her heavy round head
Warm against my chest.
But you could never sit so still, be so calm
Not when the world is right there, so close, so open.
Trembling, wobbly, you pull yourself
Up, and out, and make your way
Step by shaking, stubborn step.
You look up at me, grinning.
I try to mirror your smile, but mine doesn't stick.
I want to pull you back
Into the soft pink safety of the play pen,
But I know you'll fight me, wriggle free,
And burst through the doors – a daring
Baby-jail break.
I watch you travel, traverse the living room
And wonder how long I have
Before I'm left behind
Waving a white handkerchief

Versailles

Once, we entered the Golden Palace
You and I, and thought ourselves
The Sun Queens.

We strolled through gardens,
Fluttering leaflet fans through hedge walls
The wind whispering through the gaps in the branches
Gossip, secrets, and we listened.

We decided to take a vessel out on the lake.
'I'll row,' you said, and we embarked on our journey
Not with ladies' grace or poise, but with all the balance
Of new-born giraffes, on ballerina pointe.

Abandon all hope, all ye who enter the boat
The rocking, screaming and flailing,
Set us swaying adrift in the Versailles canal,
Cackling with laughter, howling like mad sirens,
"STOP MOVING!"

Other, more graceful birds,
Glide on the water; they stare at us
Flapping like chickens, splashing
Obliterating the tranquillity of the August afternoon.
Some songbirds giggle to see our antics,
Laughter bubbling along their chirps.

Eventually, we make it back to shore,
One wobbly leg after another.
The crowds cheer and wave at us,
Proud of our oh so regal countenances.
When you suggest riding bicycles next,
My breath catches, and I hesitate.